OUR WORLD
BARDI JAAWI
LIFE AT ARDIYOOLOON

Magabala Books

First published 2010, reprinted 2011, 2012
Magabala Books Aboriginal Corporation, Broome,
Western Australia
Website: www.magabala.com   Email: sales@magabala.com

Magabala Books receives financial assistance from the Commonwealth Government through the Australia Council, its arts advisory body. The State of Western Australia has made an investment in this project through the Department of Culture and the Arts in association with Lotterywest.

Copyright © One Arm Point Remote Community School, 2010
Copyright in individual contributions remains with the contributing artists and authors.

All rights reserved. Apart from any fair dealing for the purposes of private study, research, criticism or review, as permitted under the Copyright Act, no part of this publication may be reproduced by any process whatsoever without the written permission of the author and the publisher.

Designed by Tracey Gibbs
Printed in China at Everbest Printing Company

One Arm Point Remote Community School (WA)

Our world : Bardi Jaawi : life at Ardiyooloon / One Arm Point Remote Community School

1st ed.

9781921248238 (hbk)

One Arm Point Remote Community School (WA)

Bardi Culture Program.

Aboriginal Australians--Education--Western Australia--One Arm Point.

Curriculum enrichment--Western Australia--One Arm Point

Bardi language

371.90899915

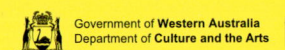

FROM THE AUTHORS AND THE PUBLISHER

From an early age, children at One Arm Point Remote Community School have grown up learning skills and gaining cultural knowledge and experiences, that many children from urban Australian schools may not have experienced. All activities in this book were carried out under culturally appropriate responsible adult supervision. We do not encourage the replication of any activities or procedures in this book without such supervision.

Indigenous people are the caretakers of their land and, as such, have the right to use their land in ways that may be prohibited in certain parts of Australia. We advise the reader to check with local authorities and to be aware of local laws before the removal or alteration of any part of their natural environment.

Aboriginal and Torres Strait Islander people are advised that this publication contains names and photographs of deceased persons. Where possible, approval has been obtained from the appropriate people to publish these names and images.

Students from One Arm Point Remote Community School

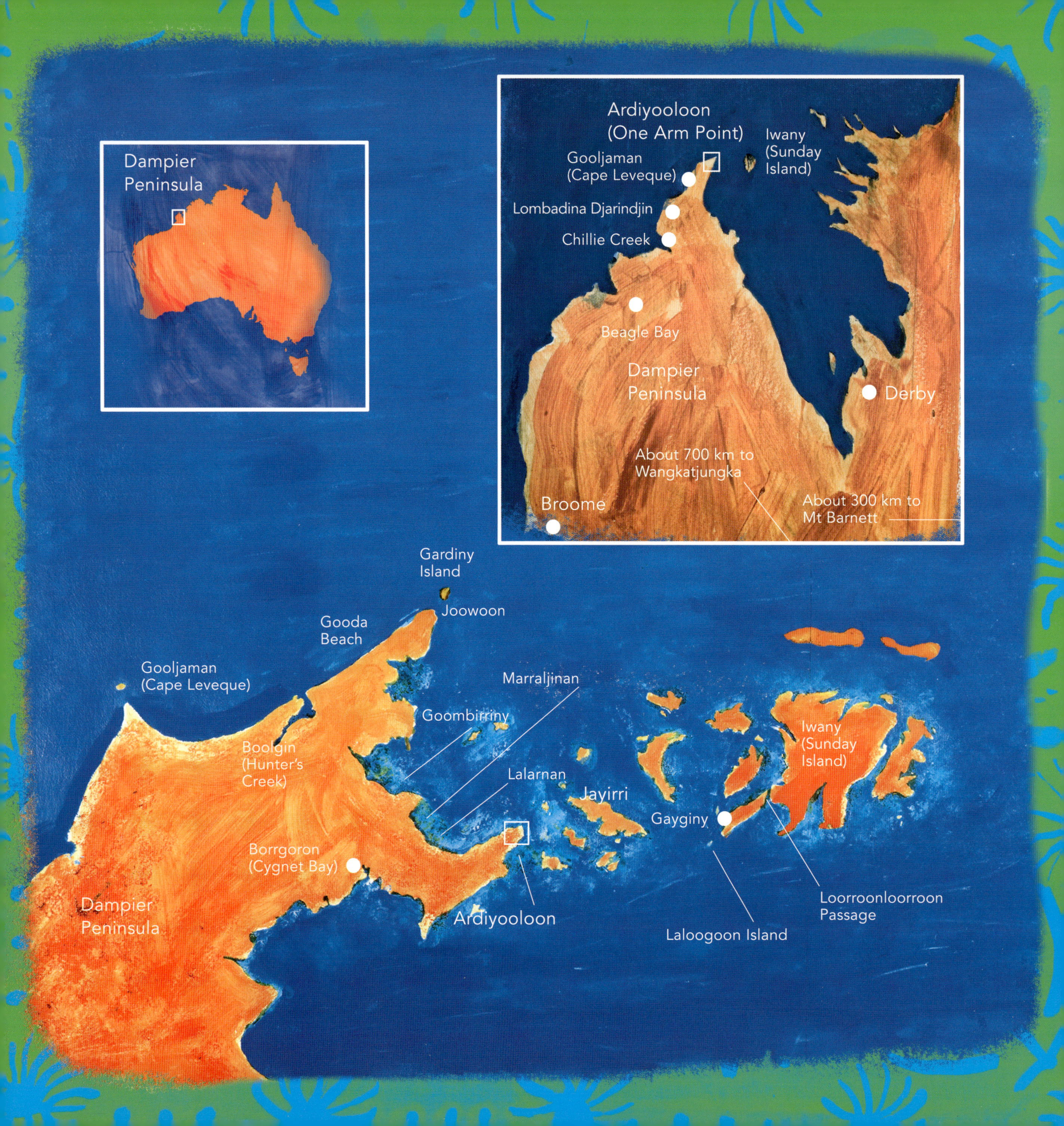

Dampier Peninsula
Ardiyooloon (One Arm Point)
Gooljaman (Cape Leveque)
Iwany (Sunday Island)
Lombadina Djarindjin
Chillie Creek
Beagle Bay
Dampier Peninsula
Derby
About 700 km to Wangkatjungka
Broome
About 300 km to Mt Barnett
Gardiny Island
Joowoon
Gooda Beach
Gooljaman (Cape Leveque)
Marraljinan
Goombirriny
Boolgin (Hunter's Creek)
Lalarnan
Jayirri
Iwany (Sunday Island)
Gayginy
Borrgoron (Cygnet Bay)
Dampier Peninsula
Ardiyooloon
Loorroonloorroon Passage
Laloogoon Island

Map labels:
- Ardiyooloon Community
- One Arm Point Remote Community School
- Airstrip
- Point Beach
- Galbarringiny (Middle Beach)
- Jologo

PRONUNCIATION GUIDE FOR BARDI WORDS

a	The sound of the 'u' in 'put' or the 'a' in 'pat'
aa	The sound of the 'a' in 'far' or 'father' (but a little bit longer)
i	The sound of the 'i' in 'sit' or sometimes the 'e' in 'set'
ii	The sound of the 'ee' in 'see' (but a little bit longer)
o	The sound of the 'o' in 'pot'
oo	Either the sound of the 'oo' in 'book' or in 'pool'
g / k	Just like the 'g' in 'go'
rd	Sounds like the 'rt' in 'party' when you say it with an American accent.
rr	Australian English doesn't have this sound – it's like the 'r' sound in Spanish, Italian or Scottish English.

In Bardi, the stress for a word always falls on the first syllable. This means it's the part of the word you emphasise most, or the one you say the loudest — like the 'fam' in 'FAMily' or the 'an' in 'ANyone'.

Ardiyooloon = AR-dee-yoo-loon

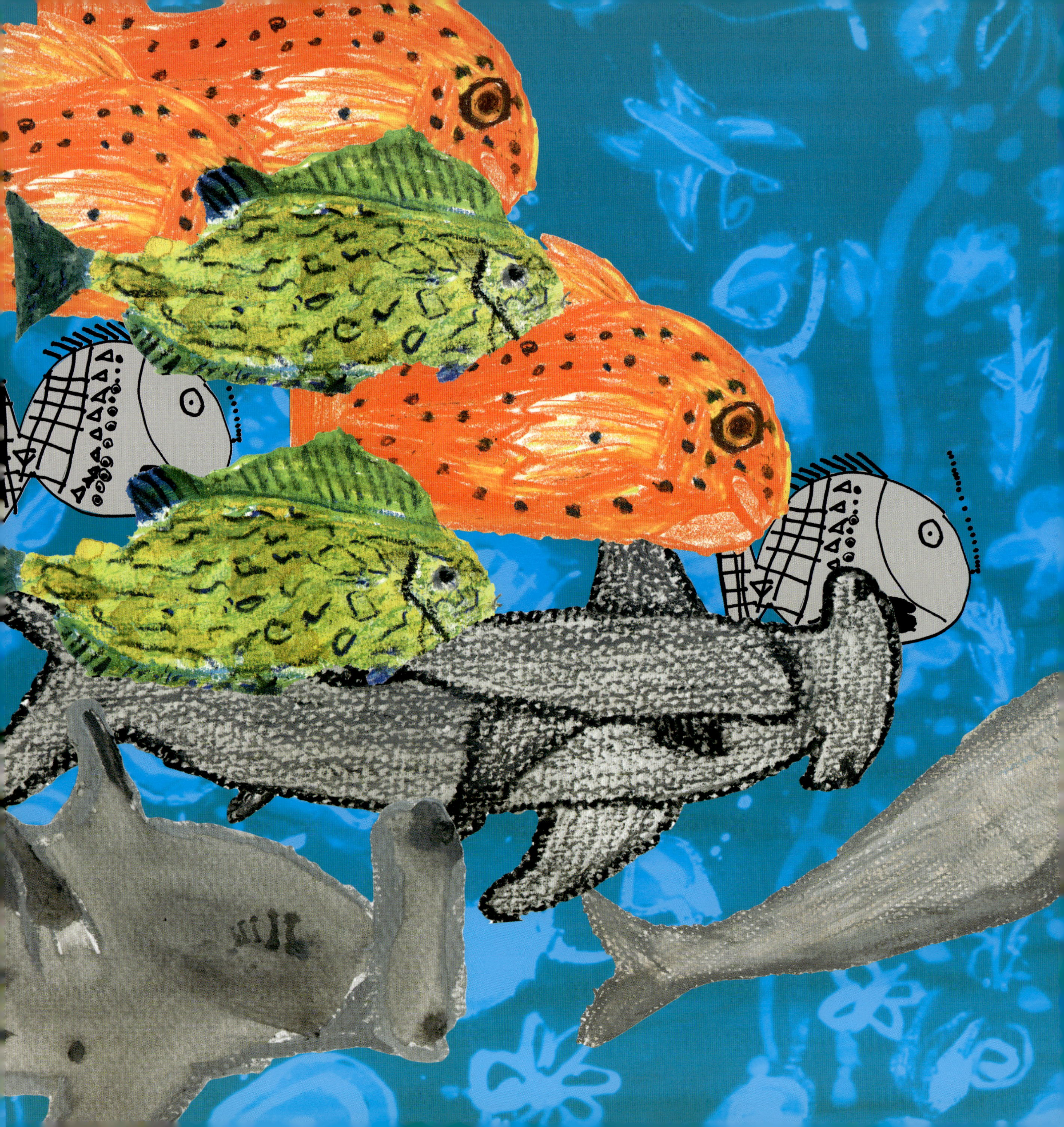

CONTENTS

Introduction	9	Bardi family ties	44
Our history	10	Fish traps	46
Spear fishing	12	Marrgaliny and Loolooloo	48
Camping at Gooda	16	Bardi Jawi Rangers	50
Cook-up at Middle Beach	20	Bardi Jaawi Seasons	51
Saltwater creatures	22	High school trip to Mt Barnett	52
Exploring the reef	24	Three boys who ate raw lizard eggs	54
Girrgij, Giido and Ganbaliny	28	Line fishing	56
Bush food	30	Camping at Gayginy	58
Fish poisoning and spearing	34	One Arm Point Culture Program	62
Our trip to Borrgoron	36	English–Bardi wordlist	63
Kangaroo and Hermit Crab	38	Acknowledgements and The Team	64
Hunting	40	Illustration credits	The end

8

INTRODUCTION

We are the descendents of a very old race: we are the Bardi Jaawi people of the Ardiyooloon community. We are saltwater people, and we carry our culture from our ancestors who lived on the surrounding islands and mainland. Our people have faced many hardships over the last century, and our community has been dispersed. Now we struggle to maintain our traditional way of life. This is why we work hard to pass our language and cultural knowledge on to our children and grandchildren for future generations.

We live on the northern tip of the Dampier Peninsula in the Kimberley Region of Western Australia. We survive off the land and the sea, and we are surrounded by crystal blue waters and white sandy beaches.

Our school is the centre of Ardiyooloon community; it has grown from the first Bardi Jaawi school in Iwany (Sunday Island) to the tin shed at Middle Beach, and to what it is today. Our Elders have a strong culture and have kept that alive. They also see the importance of education. Our school has been a successful school since the day it began, because our Elders have been watching over it, teaching respect and pride in our Bardi Jaawi culture. In this book, we share our world with you through the stories, artwork and photos that have come from the Culture Program activities we run at our school.

We want to acknowledge our Elders who have kept our culture alive and have made us strong Indigenous leaders. Without their wisdom, strength and spirit we would not be here today. We would be lost without our culture and language.

This book is dedicated to our Bardi Jaawi ancestors and our Elders from today.

One Arm Point Culture Team

OUR HISTORY

SUNDAY ISLAND MISSION

The Bardi Jaawi people, and many Indigenous people on the Dampier Peninsula, had much of their lives and their culture damaged with the arrival of pearlers and missionaries during the nineteenth century and beyond. Sunday Island Mission was established in 1899 and closed many years later in 1960. The Bardi Jaawi people used to move between the mission and the mainland. When the mission closed in 1960 the Bardi Jaawi went back to the mainland to live. They could not move to their own country. They had to live in Derby or Lombadina as no facilities were available in their own traditional area. After a number of years people began to slowly move back to their traditional lands. The government supported this movement by establishing much-needed facilities and this is how Ardiyooloon grew.

Aerial view of Ardiyooloon today.

This photograph was taken a long time ago. It is of all our great great-grandparents. They caught the fish in a large rock pool. They scared the fish into the pool when the tide was going out. They threw rocks and all the fish got into the pool. This photograph was taken at Sunday Island (Iwany) when all the Bardi people used to live at the mission.

Pop Carter's house, 1972.

Pop Carter and the first school children at Middle Beach.

THE FIRST SCHOOL AT MIDDLE BEACH

Pop Brian Carter and his family travelled from Victoria in the early 1970s to live at Ardiyooloon. It was a long, hard drive and there were no sealed roads in the north, only sand and gravel. Pop Brian and Nan Violet had six children, and the whole family lived at Middle Beach (Galbarringiny) with the other families. Their houses were made mostly of tin.

The first school was under a bough shelter, which we call a baali. Pop Brian became the first schoolteacher after he began to teach his own children and others wanted to come along to the school.

Things were difficult back then. There was little technology and although life was simple, it could be hard. People had to collect water from the old well in flour drums and jam tins.

They would get rations once a month like powdered milk, dried meat, flour and milk biscuits. They had to work hard to build and maintain the community and they were paid through rations. There were no roads and sometimes they would have to walk a long way to get something. Few people had cars. People went fishing in a dinghy, and hunted for dugong (odorr) and turtle (goorlil). They dug for fresh water at Jologo. While they built houses, they lived in tents. The houses were made out of tin and wood.

In 1974, there were twenty-five students aged from six to ten. The students sat on the clean beach sand. They used paper and pencils, and the teacher wrote on the blackboard with chalk. They were doing their lessons by correspondence through the radio.

When the kids were at school, they had to be very good or they would get the cane across their bottom. When they finished school, they collected trochus shells and they would eat the meat. School finished for kids when they were 12 years old. They were just little kids living free in the open.

SPEAR FISHING

SPEARS FOR WOMEN AND CHILDREN

We have different spears for men and women. Men's spears are longer and have wire and rod on the end. The women's spears just have a sharpened end.

We learned how to make the small spear that is used for fishing, reefing and crabbing. The old people would use these spears to feel under the reef for fish. They would then use the spear to drag the fish from the reef. When the fish came out, they would get another spear and poke it.

To make the small spear we used an axe to chop off the small bumps. We then peeled off the bark and used sandpaper to make it smooth. To make the point, we used a knife or an axe.

HOW TO MAKE A SPEAR

MATERIALS
- axe
- a hard rock
- a metre of good wood from the roots of the mangrove tree
- matches
- firewood
- sandpaper

STEPS
1. Choose a piece of wood, and peel the bark off. If it is hard to take off the bark, place the wood on a rock and hit it with the back of an axe.
2. When the bark is off, sharpen the big end of the stick with an axe. Hold the stick horizontal and chop, sharpening the end.
3. Use the wood and matches to light the fire. Place the stick into the fire to straighten the spear.
4. Finish by rubbing the stick smooth with sandpaper or a file.

iidarr = creek

ngoobiliny = squid

warrwa = shoots of mangrove trees

joongoorr = small fishing spear for women

bardag = wood

aarli = fish

ngaarraangoo = mud crabs

inamboogal = speared

FISHING AND MUD CRABBING IN THE MANGROVES

We went fishing with the girls from Beagle Bay and Wangkatjungka. We used squid for bait. The first fish caught was a good enough size for a feed. Miss Jones put sinkers and hooks on all the lines. We got no bites, so we thought it would be a good idea to try our luck at another creek but Miss Nat got bogged and the girls in the back had to get out and push. The girls in the front didn't get out and help push. When Miss Nat let the tyres down, we started to move again and drove to the creek.

Our first mud crab was found in a stream of water. Everyone gathered around for a look but it was only a small one. We found a huge mud crab but it hid away. In the end we only caught three. While we were crabbing, we collected bombies (bomb shells) and nerrite shells from the mangroves.

Climbing through the mangroves is a lot of fun. We had to be really careful not to slip and fall over when we were climbing through the roots. If you step on the shoots of the mangroves growing up from the mud, they can put a hole in your foot. When we got back to camp, Miss Jacquie put the mud crab and the fish on the fire.

13

irrol = spear

nimarl = hand

niimbal = foot

MAKING MEN'S SPEARS

When we make these spears, we get the bark off the sapling in a number of ways: by whittling it off with an axe, using a rasp to scrape it off, or using a hammer and chisel. Once the bark and all the bumps are off the spear, it is ready for straightening. Rodney and the Bardi Jawi Rangers straighten the spear in the fire. Heating up the wood makes it bend better. The big boys cut and sharpen the rods.

14

nilamarr = stone axe   jamoonyoon = tomahawk

EQUIPMENT
- straight thin wattle sapling
- tomahawk
- thin steel rod
- tie-wire
- fire
- hammer
- gloves

METHOD
1. Look for a straight wattle sapling, it must be green and fresh.
2. Choose a sapling that is the right length. Approximately 60–100cm taller than you are.
3. Cut the sapling down at ground level and let it dry overnight.
4. Next day, skin the bark off the sapling, using a tomahawk, knife, rock or hammer to loosen the bark. (Our Elders used a stone axe instead of a tomahawk.)
5. Light a fire. If the sapling has any bends, heat that section of the sapling in the flames, turning slowly. Using hands and/or feet, straighten the bend out of the sapling. Cut the thick end of the sapling with a tomahawk into a wedge shape.
6. Cut the rod into lengths. Sharpen one end of the steel rod to a point.
7. Heat the blunt end of the steel rod in the fire. Take it out of the fire using a glove. Overlap the hot blunt end of the rod and the cut end of the sapling. Hold down the rod with a hammer to burn a groove into the sapling.
8. When the rod has cooled down, hold the rod onto the spear and wrap the tie-wire tightly around the rod and sapling starting from the tip of the sapling moving down the spear.
9. This is a good spear for fishing and crabbing.

raanyji = rough, sandpaper

noorroo = fire

15

CAMPING AT GOODA

STORYTELLING WITH NAN ALMA

At night, Nan Alma was telling us about Iwany and Joowoon — twin islands which have lots of birds' eggs and bush onions. People collected shells from Gooda Beach and walked to Gooljaman to trade them for food, like flour and tea. Nan Alma told us a story about Hunter's Creek and how people used dynamite to make way for the boats to come in and pick up their supplies from Gooljaman. One man went diving under the water. He went to check the dynamite and the stick went off. All the fish floated to the surface. They were shaking the man to wake him up.

GIRLS' CAMP — EXPLORING THE REEF

We went on the reef at Gooda to catch fish. We were walking with our spears and we found lots of clam shells. The Elders teach us to only take what we need and not be greedy. We also found blue-ringed octopus, pink and purple sea slugs, and orange Spanish dancers. Spanish dancers are sea slugs that float, spin and twirl in the water like flamenco dancers.

Aunty Jacquie told us to go to the edge to catch fish for dinner. Two girls caught a bluebone. One girl picked up a pink and purple shell, but she dropped it when she saw a Spanish dancer. It landed in a pool with a trochus shell and they started to fight. The pink shell had a slug in it. Afterwards we went looking for mud crabs and oysters.

jagoorr = egg

jawal = stories

ngoolnga = trumpet shell

alngir = trochus shell

oola = water, rain   **loonggin = windbreak**

DIGGING FOR WATER

When we went to Gooda, we had a girls' camp and a boys' camp. First the Elders showed us how to make windbreaks to protect the camps from strong winds. We collected branches and dug a hole, we put the branches in and filled the hole. We put a rock next to the branches so they didn't fall over.

Then we went to a special place. We had to be quiet because it was a sacred place. Pop Peter told us that this place was an old waterhole, and we got a shell and started to dig. The hole got bigger and bigger and the sand got wetter and wetter. We dug really deep. It was good to visit that old waterhole.

> **did you know?**
>
> The old people passed the information about where waterholes are situated from generation to generation. This was very important for survival. The Elders used to dig the hole and fill their billy can. Then they covered the hole with sand, so when high tide came the salt water didn't get in. The location of the waterholes affected where people camped.

GOING FOR MUD CRABS

In the morning, Aunty Jacquie took us crabbing. Some of us went into the mangroves, while the others looked for crabs on the beach. The mangroves were really muddy and dark. We saw a mud crab, but the shell was too hard to spear. We finally got it, spearing it with a spear that was more powerful. One of the girls used all her might and cracked it in the shell.

We followed Miss Vivien out of the mangroves onto another beach where there were more crabs. A girl nearly stepped on one — it was covered in mud! She speared it between the eyes. Then we saw a bigger one. When we were walking back, we found oysters on a mangrove tree. We hit the branch and they all fell off. We sat under a tree and waited for the other kids to come out of the mangroves.

ooranybaawa = girls

amboolooo = baler shell   **biidin = waterhole**

jilangoor = blue-ringed octopus

SPEARING ON GOODA REEF

We had spaghetti and toast for breakfast, and then went searching for ghost crabs because they make great bait. The high school boys went spearing on the reef. Uncle Ashley pointed to a pool and we walked there. The pool had lots of fish, and we caught two golden-lined spinefoot and two surgeon fish. One of the boys caught six fish! We had to save our fish for supper. After we had a rest, we went for mud crabs. All the girls caught crabs, but only one of the boys caught a crab. We put all our fish in alfoil and cooked them in an earth oven, then added the crabs and had a big cook-up.

ooloor = mangrove tree

aambabaawa = boys

barrbal = golden-lined spinefoot

HOW TO DRESS A SNAKE BITE

METHOD
1. Move to the shade.
2. Rip your shirt off into pieces.
3. Wrap it around the snake bite.
4. Make sure it is tight.
5. Put the sticks on each side of the snake bite and wrap around more of your shirt.
6. Send for help and stay still.

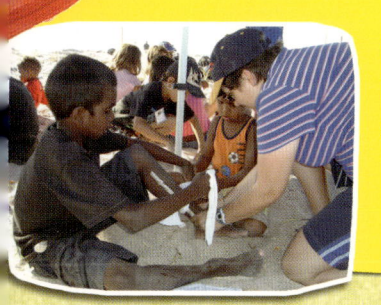

CHECK
If you survive, you have done this right.

GOAL
- If you follow these steps you should survive a snake bite.

EQUIPMENT
- A shirt and some sticks.

did you know?

HELICOPTER TREES
These trees have seeds with little rotors on them like helicopters. When you throw the seed in the air it spins around and around and comes to land gently on the ground. And that's why they are called helicopter trees.

MAKING SHIELDS

The boys learnt how to make shields with the help of Ashley, Pop Joe, Moochoo, Brusha, Pop Peter, Pop Phillip and Mr Rodney. We used axes, chisels, files and sandpaper to make the shields out of mangrove wood and helicopter trees. The mangrove wood is much softer than the wood from the helicopter tree.

Shields were used in the old days for protection when fighting. Artwork can also be painted on shields and these are used for ceremony. Only men are allowed to paint the shields and they use traditional and modern designs. Sometimes the men engrave designs on them.

marrga = shield

gambarl = surgeon fish

19

COOK-UP AT MIDDLE BEACH

BIG FEED

We had a feast at Middle Beach. After we played a game of soccer, we learnt how to make turtle kebabs. Yum! We threaded the marinated meat onto the kebab sticks and cooked them on the barbeque. Mr Rodney showed us how to make yummy satay sauce which we poured over the top of the kebabs. We cooked up fish and turtle in the earth oven and damper on the coals. While we waited for the food to cook, Miss Violet told us some old stories. We listened to the stories and had a big laugh.

did you know? Dugong and turtle are protected in certain parts of Australia but the Bardi Jaawi people have the right to hunt these animals in their traditional waters. They have been doing it for thousands of years and know how to make sure that dugong and turtle will not become endangered.

laalboo = earth oven (traditional)

gorna niyarra = sweet food

madoorr = vitamin C tree   nararr innyagal = sticky

HOW TO MAKE AN EARTH OVEN

MATERIALS
- flat stones, large and small
- wood for fire
- shovel
- damp hessian bag
- madoorr tree leaves
- fish and turtle
- foil

METHOD
1. Dig a hole about one metre deep.
2. Place the larger stones at the bottom of the hole.
3. Light a fire in the hole.
4. When the fire is going well, place the smaller stones on top of the fire to heat.
5. When the fire has burned down to coals and the rocks are hot, take out the smaller rocks.
6. Wrap turtle and fish in foil and place them on the coals.
7. Place the small, hot rocks on top of the fish.
8. Place the madoorr tree leaves on top of the rocks and cover with a damp hessian bag.
9. Fill the hole with sand. Make sure that no smoke is escaping from the hole.
10. Leave until the food is cooked, 1–2 hours.
11. Dig up and enjoy!

DAMPER

Damper is our main food. We have it for breakfast, lunch and tea. When we go camping or fishing we cook it in the hot sand but at home we cook it in a frying pan or oven. This is how you make damper:
1. Get some flour and water and squish it up. 2. Put it onto a tray and make into a shape. 3. Cook it on the coals. 4. Eat it!

One of the Bardi people's favourite tucker is what we call lanjarr, which is the turtle's breast. We put it on a metal grate (in this picture we used an old screen door) and cook it over the hot coals. It is very yummy, we scrape the meat off the shell to eat it.

gorna gija = delicious

inanggalboogara = to dig out

dambidambi = salty

moola = cooked

21

SALTWATER CREATURES

1. **Dart fish = arnangarr**
   We need to use a throw net to catch these small fish.

2. **Mangrove Jack = maarrarn**
   We catchh mangrove Jack in creeks where there are mangroves.

3. **Suckerfish = ayala**
   Suckerfish stick to the backs of dugongs, whales and sharks and hitch a ride.

4. **Longtom = jamalal**
   These fish are long and skinny, but are good eating.

5. **Spanish flag = jooloo**
   We have plenty of Spanish flag, or flake, around Ardiyooloon.

6. **Pelican = jalingmarr**
   It is believed that when pelicans fly overhead, it is a sign that someone in the community is going to conceive a baby.

7. **Trevally = raarri**
   Trevally are a good fighting fish, very strong.

8. **Saddle-tailed sea perch = inyjalngan**
   These are good eating fish. They grow very big.

9. **Golden-lined spinefoot = barrbal**
   Golden-lined spinefoot fish have plenty of fat and taste quite nice.

10. **Blue-ringed octopus = jilangoorr**
    Don't touch these, they are very dangerous.

11. **Mud crab = ngarranggoo**
    Catch these when the tide goes out. They are usually speared and cooked on the hot coals of a fire.

12. **Porcupine fish = jiilarnboo**
    Porcupine fish puff up when they are threatened.

13. **Tiger shark = gandarr**
    Tiger sharks love eating turtles and are very unpredictable. They have been known to attack outboard motors.

14. **Estuary cod = biidib**
    This cod is good to eat because it has lots of fat and flesh.

15. **Golden trevally = jirral**
    Small trevally grow very fat in the cold season.

16. Turtle = goorlil
The green sea turtle eats seagrass and other sea plants. The male turtles spend their life at sea and the female turtles come and lay their eggs on the beaches around Ardiyooloon.

17. Manta ray = ambarn
We leave these alone, we do not hunt them. We respect them and they do not hurt us.

18. Blue spotted stingray = ngoojil
Don't touch this stingray, the barb might poke you!

19. Irukandji jellyfish=
Turtles eat most jellyfish, but not Irukandji. These jellyfish have very poisonous stings and are in the ocean during the wet season.

20. Dugong = odorr
Dugong travel in family groups with the bull leading in front.

21. Bluebone = goolan
We also call these fish bluebone because they have blue bones. They are fat at Lalin time.

22. Brahminy kite = joonggilbil
Brahminy kites sit on the rocks and watch the sea. When the tide is out, they fly down to the reef and catch octopus and fish.

23. White breasted sea eagle = boongginy
This eagle swoops down over the sea and grabs fish with its strong claws.

EXPLORING THE REEF

banyjarr = clam shell

marnany = reef

LOW TIDE

When the tide is low, we walk out to the reef. There are all sorts of interesting plants and animals to look at, as well as good things to eat, including a sticky octopus!

One of the Elders, Bessie, saw a big clam shell in the water. She put a stick in the clam's mouth and pulled it from the reef on the end of a stick. She got the meat from the shell with a knife, cutting out the bottom greasy bit with the black ink and putting it to the side. We eat the mussel meat raw, pickle it or dry it. We also use it in stir-fries and curries. If we dry the meat, it lasts for a month.

To collect the oysters, we use hammers and screwdrivers to break them off the rocks. We cook oysters by putting them straight on the fire or we make oyster pancakes.

niwarda = oysters

laanyji = brown seaweed

bardag = tree

goolboo = rock, stone, money

oolarda = wooden basket

wiliwili = fishing line

OYSTER PANCAKES

We love to cook oyster pancakes after we have collected them — we make pancakes with oysters straight from the reef.

EQUIPMENT
- bowl
- containers
- spoon

INGREDIENTS
- flour
- oysters
- water

METHOD
1. Wash the oysters.
2. Mix flour into batter.
3. Add oysters to batter.
4. Scoop out spoons of batter.
5. Fry in frying pan and cook until golden brown.

25

TWO WAYS TO CATCH A MONKEY FISH

EQUIPMENT
- handful of seaweed
- 2 rocks
- 1 stick
- bucket
- handful of dead coral
- fishing line
- bait

METHOD
1. Go on to the reef when it is low tide, taking seaweed, rocks and the stick in the bucket.
2. Look for a monkey fish hole. Stuff the hole with seaweed and dead corals on top.
3. Put the stick next to the hole and put rocks around the stick to hold it in place — this will mark the hole.
4. When finished, leave until the next morning's low tide.
5. Go back and take the stick out. Using the stick, pull the seaweed and coral out.
6. If no monkey fish appears, look for another hole and try catching one with a line and bait. Be sure to look for big monkey fish holes.
7. Place your baited line down the hole. When you feel a tug, that will be the monkey fish. If it keeps tugging, pull it up quickly, and then you have caught your very own monkey fish.
8. If you can't pull the monkey fish out, gently push it down with your stick to make it move. Then pull quickly.

ralirali = quickly

bardag = stick

ganyginy = neap tide

nalan = spring (big) tide

gaadiliny = monkey fish

riiwa = hole

did you know?

Monkey fish live in holes in the reef or mud flats. They come out to feed at full tide. When we are hunting them, we block their hole with seaweed and dead coral on top. When we go back the next day and remove the seaweed and coral, the fish floats up to the surface because all the oxygen has gone.

gaara = sand

injoordij = tide which is right out

boorringinyjin = high tide

27

iina = firestick

TRADITIONAL STORY

GIRRGIJ, GIIDO AND GANBALINY

Ganbaliny and Giido were husband and wife. Every morning when they woke up, they would see the smoke of a fire.

'What is that in the air?' they asked each other.

'Let's go and look,' Giido said.

Ganbaliny agreed, and off they walked.

When they got to Girrgij's camp, they saw that a fire was burning outside a cave. They hid and watched Girrgij fly away. They followed and watched him spear fish, light a fire and cook it all. Giido and her husband still ate raw shellfish, oysters and other fish.

The Lalin season had finished when Ganbaliny said to Giido, 'We'll go and see how he makes fire.'

At night time they got up and walked to Girrgij's camp. Hiding behind a rock, they

girrgij = grey goshawk

ganbaliny = pied oystercatcher

giido = sooty oystercatcher

injidoron = husband and wife

saw him pick up firesticks. He rubbed them together, he rubbed and rubbed. He put dry grass in the fire. He put the sticks back and blew on the grass. Giido and Ganbaliny saw smoke coming out. After he lit the fire, Girrgij got up and went away to fish. Then Giido and Ganbaliny picked up the firesticks and ran away and hid them, telling each other how good they were.

When Girrgij came back to his camp, he looked for the firesticks and found nothing. He saw the tracks of the husband and wife.

'I'll go and find them', he said. Girrgij didn't know where their camp was, but he could see thick smoke rising. 'They picked up my firesticks,' he said.

He followed the smoke and saw Giido and Ganbaliny sitting at the fire cooking their food. They were cooking bush potato, bush onions and rock oysters.

Ganbaliny told his wife, 'You go and look for crabs.'

The woman walked away from the fire; she looked for rock oysters and shellfish. She picked up a lot and filled up a basket. While she was walking back, she caught more fish.

When she got back to camp, she saw her husband lying on his side and Girrgij was fighting him. He'd snuck up on her husband, while she was away, pinching him with his nails and making holes in his body.

Giido tried chasing Girrgij away. 'Why did you do this?' she asked.

'You took my fire and my firesticks but now I've got them back,' he said. Then he picked up Giido and threw her onto the slippery rocks.

Giido cried, 'I'm going. We'll eat raw fish in the future.'

Girrgij told her, 'I've got back my firesticks and this fire will burn with thick smoke forever,' he said.

People used fire from then on. Nowadays we eat cooked fish. If it wasn't for Giido and Ganbaliny we would still be eating raw food.

BUSH FOOD

ilarr = bush fruit

COLLECTING PANDANUS

The pandanus tree grows in our coastal areas. It is a very hardy plant, and it doesn't mind salt in the air. In Bardi, the fruit of the pandanus palm is called gaamba.

We went to Gooljaman to collect pandanus nuts. First we had to find pandanus trees with ripe fruit. The fruit is bright orange. We were looking for fruit that had begun to dry out, so we collected what had already dropped on the ground.

LOOKING FOR BUSH ONIONS

Bush onions are found along the beach in the soft sand. There are lots of bush onions around Ardiyooloon and our islands. When we went looking for them, we first cleaned the grassy area with our hands, and then sat down and used our feet to soften the sand. This made it easier to find them. We scooped up the sand and shook it. Some of the little brown onions dropped and some stayed in our hands. We collected the ones that had fallen and cooked them in the hot sand. We then dug them out and rubbed off the outer skin to eat the white onion. They tasted very nice, sweeter than onion, and not as strong. We call them onions because of the way they look, but they taste more like peanuts.

moola = ripe

dalboon = dry

niyalboon = bush onions

idool = pandanus tree

COOKING PANDANUS

1. Collect the pandanus fruit that has fallen.
2. Light fire and let it burn down until there are lots of coals.
3. Place the fruit on the coals and cook for 4–5 minutes.
4. Wait until the outside is burnt.
5. Take the fruit off the coals.
6. Let them cool for a minute, or bury them in the sand.
7. Place the nut into the groove of a rock or piece of hard wood.
8. Split nut with an axe.
9. Take nut out with a needle or safety pin.

Enjoy!

gaamba = pandanus nut

rirrga = coals

PANDANUS NUT RECIPE

You can use unsalted macadamia nuts if you don't have pandanus palms in your part of the country!

COD FISH WITH PANDANUS NUT BUTTER

INGREDIENTS
- 100g butter
- 2 tablespoons lemon juice
- 4 tablespoons pandanus nuts (chopped roughly)
- 4 cod fish fillets
- steamed greens, we usually use asparagus, green beans and broccoli
- lemon wedge, to serve

METHOD
1. Melt butter in a large pan over medium heat, till it is light golden in colour, (make sure you don't overdo this and burn the butter).
2. Add lemon juice and pandanus nuts and saute for 1 minute.
3. Add fish to pan and cook for 2 minutes on each side, or till it is cooked to your liking.
4. Serve fish on steamed greens with the golden butter as a sauce with a lemon wedge.

MAKING BUSH BROOMS

The Elders showed us how to make bush brooms. We use them when we go camping to keep our camp clean and tidy. In the old days, the Elders did not have shops to buy brooms so they had to make their own. This is how we made them: get special branches from the tree; cut a piece of string into three; and tie the string around the branch at the top, middle and almost down to the bottom. Now sweep the floor.

barrgay = tusk shell

jooroor = wind

SHELLS, SEEDS AND BEADS

We made our own necklaces from seeds and tusk shells the girls collected at Chillie Creek on their culture camp. Tusk shells are long and white and look like elephants' tusks. They were worn in traditional ceremonies, threaded and made into large strings of shell. To use tusk shells, just break off the closed end and then thread it onto string.

The beads used are small round seeds that come from the morning glory vine that covers the ground near Middle Beach. We also used small red seeds from a tree growing in our school ground.

Our Elders used to burn holes in each seed by placing a hot wire in the fire then burning it through the seed. We learnt how to do this on our culture day. It is a long process and nowadays we use a small drill to do this.

WINDMILLS

We make windmills from pandanus leaves. You need fresh pandanus leaves. Cut off all the spikes, fold two leaves together to make the propellers. Use a sharp stick to poke through the propellers — nowadays we use wire. To make it spin around you can blow on it or, better still, hold it against the wind. On windy days they work really well.

ardiyan = north-east wind

ayalga = north wind

FISH POISONING AND SPEARING

USING FISH POISON

Ilngam is a root from a wild bush found mostly on the islands around Ardiyooloon. Only certain islands have this plant. Our ancestors taught us about ilngam, a fish poison, and this knowledge has been passed down from generation to generation. We use this poison to kill the fish — they die from lack of oxygen and they are safe to eat. People need to get lots of fish poison to catch fish.

A BIT OF HISTORY

This photograph was taken a long time ago at Laloogoon. David Wiggan is looking for fish to eat. The fish have been poisoned and he is now in the pool putting them on his spear. He is handsome. He is thinking about the biggest mob of fish he can eat.

booroo = home

bangala = ledge

ilngam = fish poison

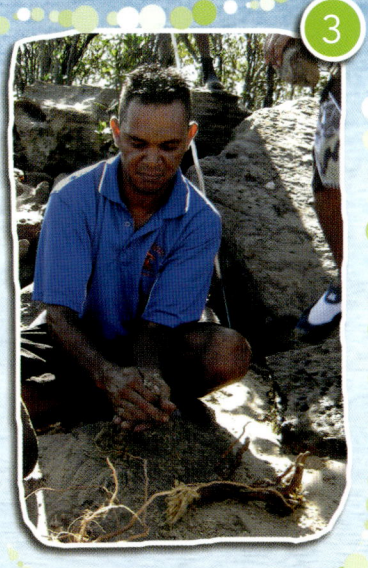

bilil = leaf

boordiji = big

HOW TO USE FISH POISON

WHAT YOU NEED
- stick or shovel
- rock
- sand
- strong bag
- spear
- bucket

METHOD
1. Find the fish poison plant and dig in the ground with a stick or a shovel for fish poison roots and pull them out. Fill a big bag with a lot of ilngam and throw away the sticks.
2. Take the roots and smash them — crush the roots with a rock.
3. Mix the fish poison with sand and put it in a bag. The sand weighs it down and it gets heavy.
4. Go off to the reef. Put the fish poison and sand in holes in the reef with ledges. That's a place where fish live.
5. Wait a little while and the fish get dizzy from the poison. The ilngam makes them feel bad, it makes the water bad so they can't breathe.
6. Then we spear them. We collect them and thread them on a spear or put them in a bucket to carry back home or to camp. We get octopus too.

yaaga = rockpool

rambin = heavy

35

OUR TRIP TO BORRGORON

BORRGORON

Our school went to Borrgoron. Borrgoron is also called Cygnet Bay. We sorted out our reefing shoes when we got there. It was a sunny day. We went on the reef, into the mangroves and visited the pearl farm.

CATCHING A FEED

The girls went on to the reef to collect rock oysters. When the tide was coming back in, the boys went spear fishing. We needed to be very quiet so we could sneak up to the fish and mud crabs. Then we threw our spears just in front of the fish. We caught a mullet, and some other fish and a stingray.

We went swimming in the big pool and fishing from the huge rocks with hand reels. We didn't catch a lot of fish because our lines keep getting caught under the rocks. But we did get a small bluebone and a Spanish flag.

When it was lunchtime, some of us cooked the fish and served it up to Pop Peter. We also cooked up the mooloo in the hot coals and the mud crab on the fire and everyone had a big feed.

We had a good day at Borrgoron!

jooloo = Spanish flag

jooboo / inji = swimming

yawiny = brown stingray

mooloo = nerite shell

aarlon iinkal = to fish

joongoon = orange spike berry tree

INTO THE MANGROVES

The little kids and the teachers went into the mangroves looking for mooloo. Mooloo are like little snails — some people call them periwinkles. While we were in the mangroves, one of the boys caught a humungous mud crab. He picked it by its swimmers and put it into a hessian bag. The kids made damper under the orange spike berry tree, and cooked up marshmallows on the fire.

PEARLING DAYS

In the 1960s, young men worked at the pearl farm at Borrgoron. They wore diver suits and used to dive for shells. People walked on the reef and picked up pearl shell and took them to Mr Brown — the owner of the pearl farm. The Brown family has owned the farm since 1946. It is the oldest family-owned pearl farm in Australia.

Pop Peter told us a story about looking for pearl shell when he was young, and worked at Borrgoron. His job was to free dive for the pearl shell. When he was diving, he had a rope around his body. When he finished collecting pearl shell he tied the rope around the bag of shells, so the people on the boat could lift it up.

We went on a tour to learn about the history of the farm, check out the big boats and try on pearl necklaces. The biggest pearl in the history of the Dampier Peninsula was found at Borrgoron.

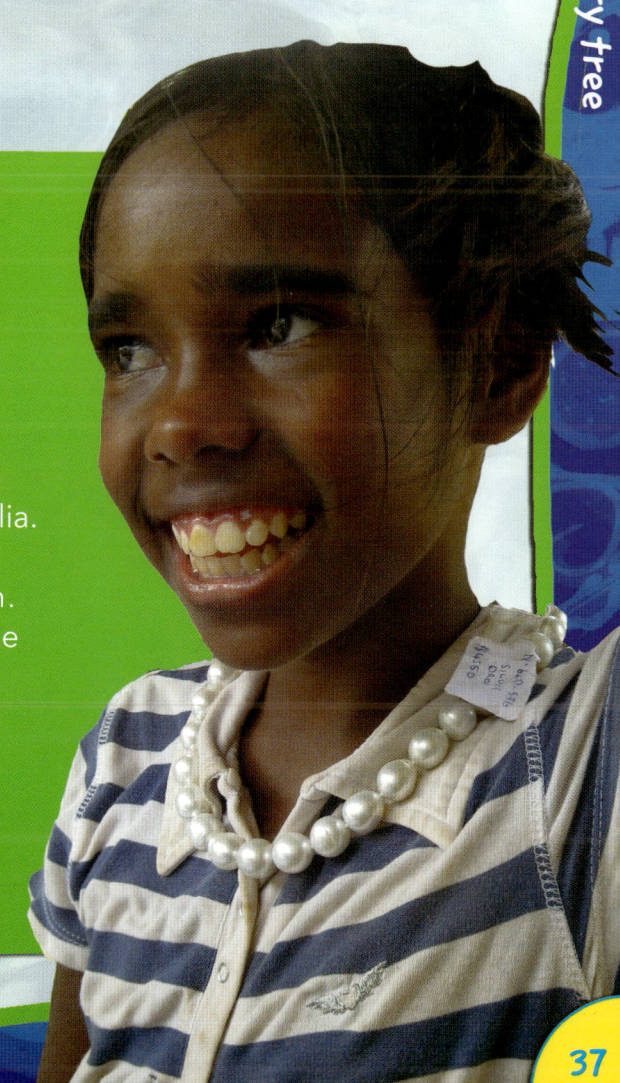

goowarn = pearl shell

37

boorroo = kangaroo

TRADITIONAL STORY

KANGAROO AND HERMIT CRAB

'Who is the fastest runner? Who wants to race me? No one can beat me I am the fastest animal here. Which one of you hermit crabs thinks they can beat me? Let's ask Snake if we can hold a race,' said Kangaroo.

So Kangaroo and Hermit Crab went to see Snake.

'Yes, you can race. We will begin the race at Cunningham Point,' said Snake.

All the animals gathered together at Cunningham Point to watch the race. There was Sea Eagle, Wedge-Tailed Eagle, Tata Lizard, Striped Lizard and Rough-Skinned Lizard.

Kangaroo and Hermit Crab lined up at the start line.

'Get ready, set, GO!!!!!' said Snake. All the animals cheered Kangaroo and Hermit Crab on.

Kangaroo was hopping fast and Hermit Crab was trailing behind, making his way slowly down the path. Kangaroo lost sight of Hermit Crab so he stopped for a break under a tree. He was lying there having a good rest, not worrying about Hermit Crab because he was such a slow runner.

'Oi, Hermit Crab where are you?' cried Kangaroo.

Hermit Crab jumped out from behind a rock in front of Kangaroo. 'Here I am Kangaroo,' he said, 'are you getting tired yet?'

Kangaroo got a big shock when he saw Hermit Crab in front of him. He must have been resting for longer than he thought. He felt ashamed that tiny Hermit Crab was beating him. 'I must go faster,' he thought.

He jumped up and hopped faster and faster, leaving Hermit Crab to follow behind. Soon he felt out of breath so he stopped for a little rest. 'Where is Hermit Crab?' he thought to himself, 'he must be a long way behind me.' 'Oi, Hermit Crab where are you?' said Kangaroo.

Hermit Crab jumped out from behind a tree in front of Kangaroo and said, 'Here I am Kangaroo. You are running so slowly, when are you going to start beating me?'

'What's going on?' wondered Kangaroo. 'I left that Hermit Crab back THERE and now HERE he is in front of me.'

larrood = hermit crab

oombala = slowly

booloobool = striped lizard

jaminybarr = fast

boongginy = white-breasted sea eagle

arriyana = wedge-tailed eagle

ganarda = tata lizard

Kangaroo began to hop along as fast as he could and left Hermit Crab crawling slowly behind. They had been racing for a very long time and were getting close to the finish line.

Kangaroo thought to himself, 'I am so tired now. I think I might lie down and have a little rest, there is no way that slow Hermit Crab can beat me.'

While Kangaroo was having a rest Hermit Crab crawled out from behind a hollow log. 'Hey Kangaroo what are you doing sleeping under that tree?' he asked.

Kangaroo jumped up, surprised to see Hermit crab standing in front of him. Kangaroo began feeling very annoyed that a little hermit crab was beating him. He thought, 'I have to win this race. I boasted to everyone how fast I am and now I am getting beaten by this tiny hermit crab.'

They were now very close to the finish line. Kangaroo was hopping as fast as he could. He was in the lead again and had left Hermit crab behind. 'See, no-one can beat me. I am the fastest. That little Hermit crab is no competition for me.'

Kangaroo was starting to feel very pleased with himself. He thought he was winning until he looked up and saw Hermit Crab in front of him!

'This can't be happening,' he shook his head. 'I am hopping my fastest and pesky Hermit Crab keeps overtaking me.'

Kangaroo looked up and saw Hermit Crab just about to cross the finish line. He began to hop faster but couldn't catch up and Hermit crab won the race. Kangaroo felt very ashamed for showing off and angry that Hermit Crab beat him.

All the animals were clapping and cheering, they did not realise Hermit Crab had played a trick on Kangaroo. Hermit crab's friends had helped him win the race by hiding along the track. Each time Kangaroo had a rest, a new hermit crab jumped out from his hiding place. Kangaroo had been tricked!

But Kangaroo learned never to show off again.

HUNTING

ANIMAL TRACKS

An animal track is the mark an animal makes when it puts its foot on the ground. Animals have different-shaped feet, so they make different tracks.

If we go hunting for goanna, we look around for their tracks and these lead us to their hiding places, either up a tree or in the tall grass. When we see turtle tracks down on the beach, we follow them up to their nest in the soft sand. We dig up the eggs and boil them.

niinbil = track

ambooriny = human

boolowman = bullock

Dog or dingo tracks

Snake tracks

Seagull tracks

Turtle tracks

40

goorrid = dingo   joorroo = snake   olorrgi = seagull

goorlii = turtle

Blue-tongue lizard tracks

Human tracks

Bull tracks

Emu tracks

Sooty oystercatcher tracks

GHOST CRAB

We learnt how to look for other signs to show us that animals have been around. Ghost crabs do not leave tracks, but they leave little balls of sand so you can see where they have been. They get their food from the sand and when they finish with it they roll it up into a ball and leave it on the surface. You can see these balls on the beach at low tide.

Kangaroo tracks

manboor = ghost crab   goodarrowin = brolga   iniini = emu

41

bardag = tree

MAKING BOOMERANGS

Nowadays, we use rifles and fishing lines to help us catch a feed. But we don't forget that the old people used to hunt with spears and boomerangs. We also tap boomerangs together to create the beat for our traditional ceremonies.

1. First, we find the tree to make boomerangs and Pop Peter cuts the wood.
2. The next step is to draw the shape on the wood. We listen carefully to Pop Peter as he tells us how to draw the boomerang and cut the wood.
3. We cut into the wood slowly, following the shape of the boomerang.
4. We make it thinner and try to form the boomerang shape.
5. Then we use the file to smooth out the boomerang.
6. Now we have a boomerang that we use for hunting birds, kangaroo and goanna.

bardajana goorlingan = to hunt

gayoor = smooth

irrgil = boomerang

girrgirr = to cut

ngalamanka = to listen

43

BARDI FAMILY TIES

BARDI KINSHIP TERMS

In Bardi lessons we learn kinship words:
- We call our father gooloo.
- We call our father's father galoongoordoo (galoo for short) and our mother's father nyami.
- We call our mother birrii.
- We call our mother's mother gamani and our father's mother goli.
- We call our father's brother gooloo too.
- We call our father's sister irrmoor.
- We also call our mother's sister birrii.
- We call our mother's brother gaarra.
- Our sister is called marrir.
- Our brothers are called babili.
- The cousins from our uncle on our mother's side are called jaal.
- The cousins from our aunty on our mother's side are called marriborl.
- The cousins from our aunty on our father's side are called jaal.
- The cousins from our uncle on our father's side are called marriborl.

44

BARDI KINSHIP CHART

- **GRANDFATHER (father's side)** — galoongoordoo (gooloo for short)
- **GRANDMOTHER (father's side)** — goli
- **GRANDMOTHER (mother's side)** — gamani
- **GRANDFATHER (mother's side)** — nyami

- **UNCLE (father's side)** — gooloo
- **AUNT (father's side)** — irrmoor
- **FATHER** — gooloo
- **MOTHER** — birrii
- **AUNT (mother's side)** — birrii
- **UNCLE (mother's side)** — gaarra

- **BROTHER/SISTER** — marrirborl
- **COUSIN** — jaal
- **BROTHER** — babili
- **YOU** — NGAYOO
- **SISTER** — marrir
- **BROTHER/SISTER** — marrirborl
- **COUSIN** — jaal

- **FATHER'S SON** — aala
- **MOTHER'S DAUGHTER** — bo

FISH TRAPS

TYPES OF FISH TRAPS

There are two kinds of fish traps. One is a fish trap with rock walls and the other is a small reef pool. The fish swim into the rock wall fish trap when the tide comes in. When the tide goes out, the fish are trapped.

With the small reef pool, people circle around the fish throwing rocks and coral, and splashing sticks to scare them into the pool. When the tide goes out, it is easy to see the fish in the pool and spear them.

ABOUT FISH TRAPS
told by Jessie Sampi

I am going to tell you a story about fish traps.

Our grandfather used to take us to catch fish in fish traps. First, he used to fix the trap by adding spinifex grass and straightening the rocks. Then he would go back home. Next morning he would say, 'Come on, let's go fishing!' We used to jump into the water and splash around with our arms so that the fish would go to one place.

Then we waited for the tide to go out. Usually lots of fish had gone inside the fish trap. Then we went home with lots of fish to cook. We'd go to sleep with full stomachs after our grandfather fixed the fish trap.

ninganyboo = armpit

oowa nimarla = little finger

bootoo = camp

noongonyi = palm

46

mayoord = rock-wall fish trap

FIXING THE FISH TRAP

We fix up the fish traps that the people made a long time ago so fish will swim into them. We help rebuild them by making the traps taller and adding more rocks.

There is a fish trap at Lalarnan. The rocks had fallen down so we went there to put them back up. We put gloves on our hands, because the rocks are sharp and we were worried that a stonefish might poke our hand, or a crab might bite us.

The fish swam into the trap when the tide came in. When the tide went out, we speared all different types of fish — mullet, trevally and squid. Some of the older boys learned how to spear fish. They speared a stingray, a big mullet and a crab.

While we waited for the tides to change, Maureen taught the kids how to make rafts. We went to look for sticks and for the spotted-leaved red mangrove that grows on the foreshore. When we had collected the pieces, we made little rafts.

NIMARL GAME

told by Nancy Issac

On Sunday Island, people played this finger game with their children. They started off with the palm — their camp, and finished up in the armpit — the cave. This is just a little story.

People used to leave their things in camp — which is the palm of hand
They went with fishing lines to catch fish — the little finger
They went to the reef to collect shell — ring finger
They went looking for turtle — middle finger
Then they went walkabout — around and around the palm
They went back to their camp and cooked their fish — palm
They went looking for water — above the elbow
In the cool of the afternoon, they went walking, looking for fruit on the scrubby hill.
They collected fruit; pink fruit, little white juicy fruit, yams…all kinds of fruit. They looked out for boats from the top of the hill — top of head
They went back home, rested for a while and dropped off to sleep — palm
They went back to camp. At nightfall, they went to sleep. When they were fast asleep, big clouds came. Rain poured down and thunder woke them up.
Then they ran to the cave and went inside — tickle under the armpit!
It's a good little story.

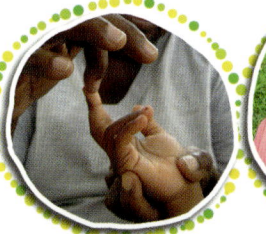

ayin = stick fish trap

biindoon = red mangrove

jaalinymarr = thumb

niyaloonggoon = elbow

47

TRADITIONAL STORY

MARRGALINY AND LOOLOOLOO

Loolooloo and Marrgaliny went around together like brothers. They got their food together. They went looking for water together. They were always together. The married turtle season was coming, and they started hunting for turtle. On the drifting tide they saw the married turtle and started to argue who was going to spear it.

'I saw the turtle first' yelled Loolooloo.

'No, I saw it first' yelled Marrgaliny.

Their argument got bigger. They kept arguing. They got cheeky and started to hit each other. Then they picked up their spears. Marrgaliny was really angry and was whacking Loolooloo really hard. Loolooloo picked up his shield and hit Marrgaliny with it.

Marrgaliny was knocked into the water. When Loolooloo came to his senses he looked around but could not find Marrgaliny. He looked in the water and could only see blood — no Marrgaliny.

'That must be Marrgaliny's blood in the water,' said Loolooloo.

Loolooloo dropped his shield and jumped into the water. He swam away.

marrgaliny = hammerhead shark

looloolo = grey-nurse shark

oondoord = married turtle

> **MARRIED TURTLE SEASON** — *did you know?*
> Lalin is the turtle hunting season. People call it 'married turtle season' because it is the mating season for turtles. It gets hot and humid during lalin, the build-up to the wet. Winds shift from westerly to strong north-westerly. Tropical storms come from the north-west at the end of Lalin and they bring rain.

Marrgaliny had turned into the hammerhead shark. That's why we gave Marrgaliny, the hammerhead shark his name — because he was hit and whacked with a shield. You can still see the shape of the shield in Marrgaliny's head.

Looloolo turned himself into a large grey-nurse shark and now the Bardi people call the grey-nurse shark, Looloolo.

These days you can still find Looloolo swimming around sandbanks when people are hunting for married turtle. When people are hunting near sandbanks, the oldest man on board dives into the water and looks around for Looloolo. When he sees the shark he dives down and rubs its head. Then shouts 'watch out for iiwala he'll come' (watch out! look after my son/nephew — who is diving for turtle, keep away the other sharks).

When the people on the boat look down they can see Looloolo's fin. He is swimming around, keeping a watch for other cheeky sharks that might come.

Looloolo is the grey-nurse shark — big long and docile. He picks people up who are drifting in the water and takes them back to their country. To thank the Looloolo people put balalagoord (wattle) leaves and white stones on his head and then send him back,

'Uncle you can go now, look out for us next time,'
they say to Looloolo.

49

BARDI JAWI RANGERS

WHO ARE THEY?

The Bardi Jawi Rangers work in Ardiyooloon. They tag turtle and dugong and track where they go. They catch and cook-up turtle and cook it in a traditional earth oven.

Bardi Jawi Rangers help out on culture days and camps. They get the shade and the firewood. They help us make spears and take us on bush fruit tours. They teach us the right way to clean up the community. They look after the islands and Ardiyooloon community.

> We, the Bardi Jawi Rangers are formed from the coastal tribe groups, Bardi (land) and Jaawi (island) which consists of six clan groups. Our culture and tradition is based on the land and sea management of caring for country and maintaining our land and sea. Local knowledge about the land and sea has been passed down from our ancestors. We are saltwater people and in our law the ocean is our provider on seasonal and traditional methods. In return we look after it by protecting, preserving and maintaining all its biodiversity and species in our country. We have been a team for more than three years and work closely with our old people and steering committee.

did you know?

JAWI OR JAAWI?
Indigenous Australian languages are oral languages. Linguists worked out a way to write the Bardi language using English. Since then, Bardi speakers have made changes to this way of writing. That is why there are still some differences in the spelling of some Bardi words, like Jawi and Jaawi.

gaarra = sea

booroo = country

iinalang = island

50

BARDI JAAWI SEASONS

We have six seasons in our Bardi Jaawi calendar. Our seasons are based on the changes in our weather, what the plants and animals are doing and how fat the fish are. Some of our seasons are very short and may only last a few weeks.

ardi = north
alanga = south
baanarr = east
goolarr = west

MANKAL — the wet • monsoons • turtle hunting ends • move inland

NGALADANY — hot, humid • end of the wet • no wind • no fruit • move very little

IRRALBOO — hot, windless, then breezes and rain • king tides • good reefing • bush fruit • fat goannas and kangaroos

BARRGANA — cold season • strong SE winds • dugong hunting • fish are fat

JALALAY — short warming-up season • low tides • good reefing • stingrays are fat • west winds

LALIN — build-up to wet • hot, humid • turtle hunting season • close to coast

Inner wheel: JAN, FEB, MAR, APR, MAY, JUN, JUL, AUG, SEP, OCT, NOV, DEC — wet / dry

HIGH SCHOOL TRIP TO MT BARNETT

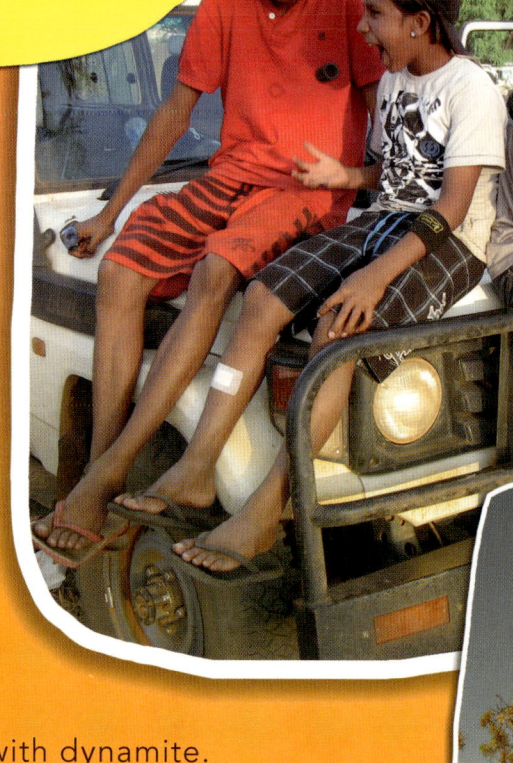

OUR JOURNEY THERE

The high school kids went to Mt Barnett to attend the Kimberley Aboriginal Law and Cultural Centre (KALACC) festival. Mt Barnett is a long way from Ardiyooloon. We left early one morning and took the back track out onto the highway. Then we turned north and headed to Derby, passing all the bridges and crossing the Fitzroy River and turning onto the Gibb River Road.

Mt Barnett is about 300 kilometres up the Gibb River Road which is mainly dirt. On the way, we saw a sign that read King Leopold Ranges, also known as Mulliewindie. Further along, we saw Queen Victoria's head. This was two huge limestone rocks which looked like the face of Queen Victoria. The head was made by blowing up part of the mountain range with dynamite.

Later on in the afternoon, we finally reached Mt Barnett. We set up camp, next to the river and had fresh fish every day for lunch and dinner.

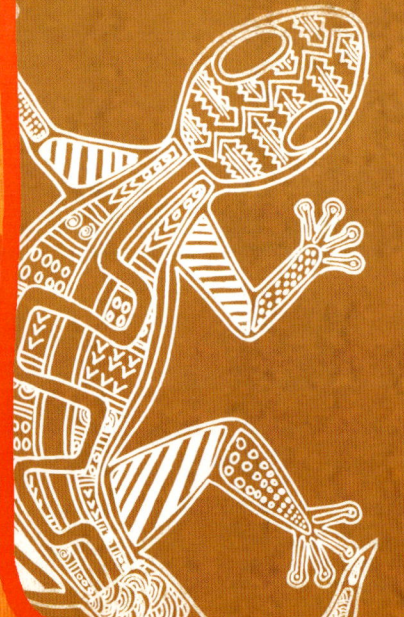

MEETING

The high school kids represented the Ardiyooloon community at two big meetings. We attended the Kimberley Land Council (KLC) and the KALACC annual general meetings. We presented silk screened tablecloths to the chair of KLC, KALACC and the traditional land owners. They were very pleased that we came and thanked us for the presents.

inoomoogarij = to make

ngannganj inawagal = to talk

imboorr inyjoogal = to paint each other

ART AND DANCE

The Bardi dancers performed, and Uncle Mooch painted up the boys. We had to dance the ilma. We danced in front of about 1000 people and we all got paid $100 each for dancing. We also watched dances from all over the Kimberley. The dancers came from the Fitzroy Valley, Mt Barnett, Kununurra and Bidyadanga.

We went to the language meeting to sell some of the silkscreen art we had made at our school. We also put together a display of our culture books for people to come and look at.

We joined in art and music activities and two of the boys learnt how to play the didgeridoo. One of the girls painted a sunset on canvas and Mr Dowling painted circles. We stayed there until it was time to have lunch.

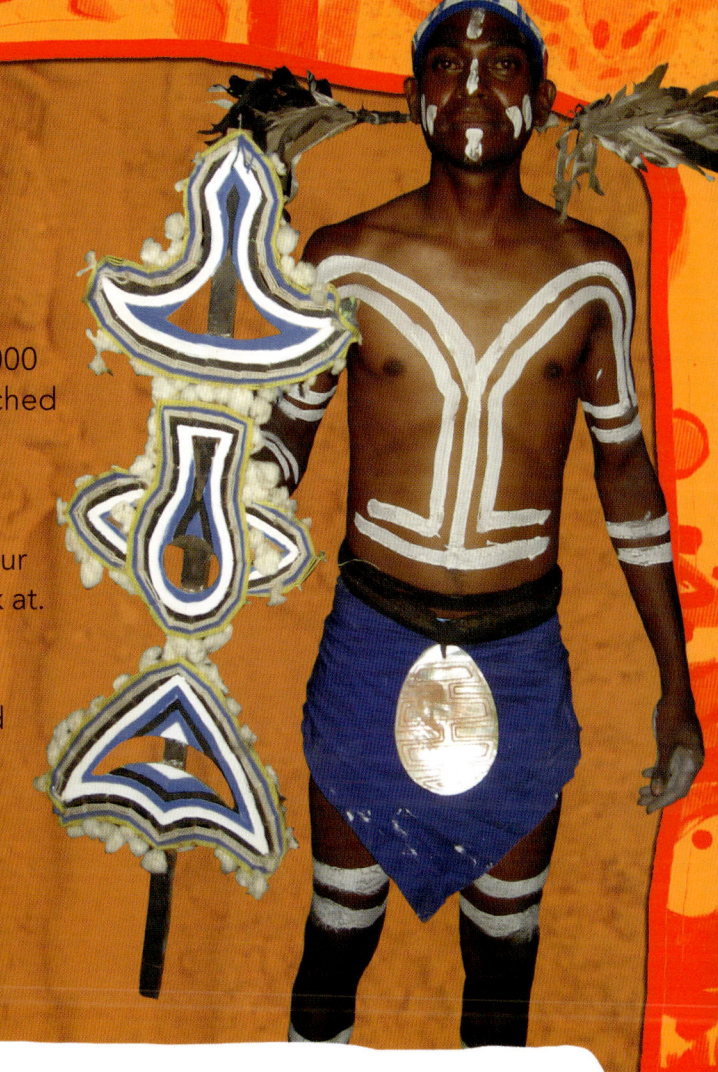

SWEET WATER FUN

In our free time we went swimming at Manning Gorge. We listened to Mr Dowling tell us some rules, then we all raced into the water to get the floating tyres first. All the boys played a catch game, and some of the kids decided to fish. One boy caught a big freshwater bream and Miss Vivien caught a barramundi, but it fell down the bank and swam away free.

darr ingarrmarinyjil = to meet

gooran inkalgal = playing

garnka = raw   manyjal = hungry

goolooman = frill-necked lizard

mayala = goanna

TRADITIONAL STORY

THREE BOYS WHO ATE RAW LIZARD EGGS

There were three boys. They went hunting for blue-tongue lizard, frill-necked lizard and little goannas. They took plenty of dogs with them.

The youngest one got hungry.

He asked the bigger boys for food. 'I'm hungry. Can I eat the eggs of the blue-tongue lizard?' he asked.

'Yes, you can eat them if you are hungry,' the two other boys said.

They cut the lizard and gutted it. They got its eggs out and ate them raw.

As they went on. They saw little clouds appear in the sky. They saw that the cloud was getting bigger. It rained. It rained lots and lots.

They ran. 'Let's hide under that tree from the rain,' they said.

It was still raining, and they were getting cold. They ran for a dry place, but there was nothing. The rain was getting so heavy. It pulled their feet into the sand, which had become soft from the rain.

The ground was getting softer. It sucked their feet in. They went further and further into the sand. They sank and couldn't get out.

They sank forever and disappeared. They hadn't listened to what the old people told them. They wanted to please themselves. The old people had told them, 'You are not allowed to eat raw food when you collect it.'

That's the way it happens when you go against the old people. When you eat raw lizard eggs, you sink into the sand and never come out.

iila = dog

ardan = clouds

ngoorboo = soft

loongoord = blue-tongue lizard

55

LINE FISHING

ayala = morning slack tide

LOOKING FOR BAIT

We went to Goombirriny to collect bait. We separated into groups. Each group took a bucket for their bait. Maureen and Dorothy taught us the Bardi names for the different baits and what we can catch with them. We use throw nets to catch small fish like big eye, which is good for catching trevally and mangrove Jack. We search the rocks for different shell bait. On the reef we get octopus, we spot them when they are out of their hiding places. Some of the kids are brave and pick up the octopus, others get frightened of its sticky tentacles.

FISHING WITH HANDLINES

We went fishing with handlines. We see our parents, grandparents, uncles and aunties using handlines all the time and want to copy them, we beg to have a go. This is why all the kids are good at throwing handlines, we were taught from an early age. Kelly caught two blue bone. For lunch we cooked up the bluebone on the fire.

langar = bait

iwooloongan = incoming tide

HOW TO COOK STUFFED FISH

WHAT YOU NEED
- alfoil
- knives
- cutting board
- cleaned and gutted fish
- tomato
- onion
- lemon pepper

METHOD
1. Slice onion and tomato.
2. Put onion and tomato into fish belly.
3. Sprinkle fish with lemon pepper seasoning.
4. Wrap fish in alfoil.
5. Bake on the coals for 3–4 minutes on both sides.

HERMIT CRAB RACES

After fishing we had hermit crab races. The crabs raced from the centre of a circle to the outside. It was good fun. We find hermit crabs at the edge of the mangroves and the beach area. They hide away among rocks, leaves and dry grass.

lyoordin = outgoing tide

babili = little tide

57

CAMPING AT GAYGINY

GETTING THERE

We couldn't wait to go to school because we were going on a camp to Gayginy on Sunday Island. Gayginy is a holiday camping area for the Bardi Jaawi people.

A little boat picked us up from Point Beach and took us to the big boat. It took about ten minutes to get across. The camping area hadn't been used for a long time so we had to pull out the grass to make a clear path to the tents. Our Elders used to camp here so we camped in the same place.

We set the tents up behind the sand dunes to make a windbreak and to keep us safe from crocodiles that might come in the night.

goojoo = grass

A DEADLY DAY FISHING AT GAYGINY

Don't talk to me, fish biting my line.

Check out this trevally. I know what I'm having for dinner.

When we went fishing on Gayginy, we used handlines and squid for bait. There are many kinds of fish we catch off the beach such as mangrove Jack, bluebone, queenfish, trevally, and Spanish flag. It was a nice sunny day for fishing. Some of the kids were lucky and caught fish that were cooked on the fire at the camp.

danggoorroo = night

58

baali = bough shelter   maarrarn = mangrove Jack

HOW TO MAKE A BOUGH SHELTER

We were divided up into six groups. It was a competition to see which group could make the best bough shelter. Elders, Bessie and Irene were the judges. Each group had to give their bough shelter a Bardi name.

EQUIPMENT
- four forked sticks
- axe
- shovel
- 8–10 straight sticks
- bushes or grass
- rope or string

METHOD
1. Stand forked sticks in holes and cover with sand.
2. Place four straight sticks between forked sticks.
3. Tie down sticks with rope or string.
4. Place remaining sticks evenly between forked sticks and tie down.
5. Put bushes or grass on top of bough shelter for shade.

birrinyan = queenfish

jabiyang = sawfish

indidi = blue crab

LOORROONLOORROON PASSAGE

On the second day of our camp, we went for a hike across the Loorroonloorroon Passage. On the way we listened to one of the Elders tell stories of growing up on Sunday Island. They had to go across the Loorroonloorroon Passage to go to school. If the tide was low they could walk, but if it was high they had to swim across. Everyone talked Bardi in those days and there was no English. When the mission closed, all the families were moved south to Djarindjin and over to Derby. The Bardi language faded away then because the people were not allowed to speak it at school or in the hostel where they stayed.

It was a very hot day and we had to rest many times. When we stopped, everybody told more stories. On the way back, we lit a fire to clear the overgrown trail behind us. Later, as we sat around the campfire, we could see the glow of the fire upon the hill in the distance.

jandooloo = mullet

gigillongga = parrotfish

goonjala = flathead

mirrjany = octopus

NIGHT FISHING

After dark, we went fishing on the reef just below Gayginy. With torches and spears, we collected Spanish flag, big-eye, golden-lined spinefoot and flathead for bait. We speared a red octopus which no one had ever seen before. Then we went to the drop-off and cast our lines.

We saw a few squid swimming on the surface, a crocodile on the island out in front and a shark chasing some fish. We all had bites, but we only caught a Spanish flag.

The tide started to come back in so we walked back to camp. We like to go spearing at night because it is more fun. You catch more fish then because they can't see your shadow. It is also nice and quiet, and there are no kids to scare them away with their big noise, swimming and splashing.

linygoorr = crocodile

ILMA

Pop Joe asked the boys if they wanted to dance Ilma, our Bardi corroboree. We were excited to learn how. We were painted up with white and grey paint. Bushes were collected and a hole dug to put them in. We stood behind the bushes and copied Salwyn. Pop Joe and Nan Bessie sang and Pop Joe played music with a tin cup and spoon. The boys danced Ilma and we felt proud and happy. Salwyn also danced the Ngaarri dance and made us laugh. The Ngaarri dance is a spirit dance where the Elders tell stories about the Ngaarri spirit chasing them to stop the kids from wandering into the wrong areas. Salwyn got dressed up as a Ngaarri to scare the children, but they all thought it was good fun.

ilma = corroboree

mooyoon = morning

ONE ARM POINT CULTURE PROGRAM

The One Arm Point Culture Program was initiated in 2008 when Bardi Jaawi Elders and community members asked for a culture program to be developed within the school. The Elders have always played an integral role in the school community, and they wanted to find ways to pass on their knowledge and ensure that Bardi Jaawi traditional culture and language was kept alive for future generations.

Earlier in 2006, the Bardi Jaawi people had won a long battle when the Federal Court ruled that they had native title rights over their land, sea, reef and islands. Native title is an acknowledgement by the Australian Government that some Indigenous people have rights to land that comes from their traditional law and long connection to country. It was awarded to the Bardi Jaawi people because of their strong connection to country.

The One Arm Point Culture Program is managed by a Culture Team made up of Elders, community members and school advisors. The program has now become one of the most important parts of the school's curriculum, and it has won state and national education and reconciliation awards for its commitment to cultural maintenance.

Each fortnight, the school runs activities such as spear making, dancing, storytelling, cooking bush tucker, traditional fishing practices, Bardi language, camps and visits to country. This culminates in a cultural concert that is held at the end of each school term. An old classroom has been set up at the school as a cultural history museum and houses a record of the cultural learning journeys.

The integration of the Bardi Jaawi traditional ways of life with the contemporary school curriculum has produced a vibrant, energetic and rich learning environment. It has empowered the youth with cultural knowledge, brought family groups together and worked towards community harmony.

ENGLISH–BARDI WORDLIST

armpit = ninganyboo
bait = langar
baler shell = ambooloo
big = boordiji
blue crab = indiidi
bluebone = goolan
blue-tongue lizard = loongoord
boomerang = irrgil
bough shelter = baali
boys = aambabaawa
brolga = goodarrowin
brother = babili
bullock = boolooman
bush fruit = ilarr
bush onions = niyalboon
camp = booroo
chop (to) = girrgirr
clam shell = banyjarr
clouds = ardan
coals = rirrga
cod = balgarraniny
cooked food = moola
corroboree = ilma
country = booroo
cousins (from father's brother) = marriborl
cousins (from father's sister) = jaal
cousins (from mother's brother) = jaal
cousins (from mother's sister) = marriborl
creek = iidarr
crocodile = linygoorr
cut (to) = girrgirr
dad = iiwala
dart fish = arnangarr
delicious = gorna gija
dig out (to) = inanggalboogara
dingo = goorrid
dog = iila
dry = dalboon
dugong = odorr
earth oven = laalboo
east = baanarr
egg = lagoorr
elbow = niyaloonggoon
emu = iniini
estuary cod = biidib
fast = jaminybarr
father = gooloo
father's brother = gooloo
father's father = galoongoordoo (galoo)
father's mother = goli
father's sister = irrmoor

finger (little) = oowa nimarla
fire = noorroo
firestick = iina
fish = aarli
fish (to) = aarlon iinkal
fish poison = ilngam
fishing line = wiliwili
fish trap (rock-wall) = mayoord
fish trap (stick) = ayin
flathead = goonjala
food (sour) = liinyja
food (sweet) = gorna niyarra
foot = niinbal
frill-necked lizard = goolooman
ghost crab = manboor
gill = nimarryi
girls = ooranybaawa
goanna = mayala
golden-lined spinefoot = barrbal
grass = gooljoo
grey goshawk = girrgij
grey-nurse shark = loolooloo
hammerhead shark = marrgaliny
hand = nimarl
head = nalma
heavy = rambin
hermit crab = larrood
hole = riiwa
home = booroo
human = ambooriny
hungry = manyjal
hunt (to) = bardajana goorlilngan
husband and wife = injidoron
island = iinalang
jellyfish = joomoolgoorr
kangaroo = boorroo
leaf = bilil
ledge = bangala
listen (to) = ngalamanka
longtom = jamalal
make (to) = inoomoogarij
mangrove (spotted-leaved, red) = biindoon
mangrove Jack = maarrarn
mangrove shoots = marrma
mangrove tree = ooloor
manta ray = ambarn
married turtle = oondoord
married-turtle season = Lalin
meet (to) = darr ingarrmarinyjij
money = goolboo
monkey fish = gaadiliny
morning = mooyoon
mother = birrii

mother's brother = gaarra
mother's father = nyami
mother's mother = gamani
mother's sister = birrii
mud crab = ngarranggoo
mullet = jandooloo
nephew = iiwala
nerite shell = mooloo
night = iidanngoorroo
north = ardi
octopus (blue-ringed) = jilangoor
octopus = mirrjany
orange spike berry tree = joongoon
oysters = niwarda
paint each other (to) = imboorr inyjoogal
palm (of hand) = noongonyi
pandanus nut = gaamba
pandanus tree = idool
parrotfish = gilgillongga
pearl shell = goowarn
pelican = jalingmarr
pied oystercatcher = ganbaliny
place = booroo
playing = gooran inkalgal
porcupine fish = jiilarnboo
queenfish = birrinyan
quickly = ralirali
rain = oola
raw = garnka
reef = marnany
ripe = moola
rock = goolboo
rockpool = yaaga
rough = raanyji
saddle-tailed sea perch = inyjalngan
salty = dambidambi
sand = gaara
sandpaper = raanyji
sawfish = jabiyang
sea = gaarra
seagull = olorrgi
seaweed (brown) = laanyji
shield = marrga
sister = marrir
slippery = gayoor
slowly = oombala
smooth = gayoor
snake = joorroo
soft = ngoorboo
son = iiwala
sooty oystercatcher = giido
south = alanga

Spanish flag = jooloo
spear (for men) = irrol
spear (for women) = joongoorr
speared = inamboogal
squid = ngoobiliny
stick = bardag
sticky = nararr innyagal
stingray (blue-spotted) = ngoojil
stingray (brown) = yawiny
stone = goolboo
stone axe = nilamarr
stonefish = jiyaroong
stories = jawal
striped lizard = booloobool
suckerfish = ayala
surgeon fish = gambarl
swimming = joobool injij
talk (to) = nganngan inamagal
tata lizard = ganarda
thumb = jaalinymarr
tide (big spring) = nalan
tide (high) = boorrnginyjin
tide (incoming) = iwooloongan
tide (little) = bola
tide (morning, slack) = ayala
tide (neap) = ganyginy
tide (outgoing) = lyoordin
tide (which is right out) = injoordij
tiger shark = gandarr
tomahawk = jamoonyoon
track = niinbil
tree = bardag
trevally (brassy) = raarri
trevally (golden) = jirral
trochus shell = alngir
trumpet shell = ngoolnga
turtle = goorlil
tusk shell = barrgay
uncle = iiwala
vitamin C tree = madoorr
water = oola
waterhole = biidin
wedge-tailed eagle = arriyana
west = goolarr
white-breasted sea eagle = boongginy
wind (before rain) = irrbooljoolj
wind (north) = ayalga
wind (north-east) = ardiyan
wind (north-west) = banijoon
wind (westerly) = alnban
wind = jooroor
windbreak = loonggin
wood = bardag
wooden basket = oolarda

ACKNOWLEDGEMENTS

One Arm Point Remote Community School would like to acknowledge and thank the Ardiyooloon Community for their support and contribution to its Culture Program.

Thank you to Robyn Wells, consultant artist, for the work she did with the children and their artwork and thanks to Claire Bowern and Laura Kling for their language translation and pronunciation guide.

We would also like to recognise the team at Magabala Books for their hard work and dedication in bringing this book to publication.

Thanks to the Kimberley Aboriginal Law and Culture Centre (KALACC) for their continued support; and to the Yulgibar Trust and Myer Foundation for their financial support.

Thanks to the Bardi Jawi Rangers (Kimberley Land Council) for permission to reproduce their logo and text.

Magabala Books would also like to thank and acknowledge the support of Rio Tinto and The Fouress Foundation.

THE TEAM

SCHOOL CULTURE TEAM
Jacquie Hunter, Rhona Bin Hitam-D'Antoine, Peter Hunter, Dorothy Davey, Rodney Maher, Jefferey Parriman, Estelle Xavier, Samantha Price, Maureen Hunter, Vivien Hunter, Jacinta Bedford, Kerry Smith, Lizzy Payne, Gary Smith.

COMMUNITY ELDERS
Violet Carter, Bessie Ejai, Jessie Sampi, Peter Hunter, Alma Ejai.

SCHOOL STAFF
Stephen Price (Principal), Natalie Oxbrow, Karen Jones, Amy Hartwig, Joshua Murphy, Keith Bedford, Jenny Mcarthy, Tanya Rosendorf, Erin Smith, Richard Dowling, Rhyz Maher, Shekima Ejai, Bartholomew Clancy, Lloyd Morris, Belinda Pushong, Hayley Smalley.

PHOTOGRAPHERS
Natalie Oxbrow, Richard Dowling, Brian Carter.

THE CHILDREN
Billi-Joh Angus, Bonnita Angus, Jah-Sali Angus, Joshua Angus Jnr, Kasey Angus, Raymond Angus, Zihan Angus, Anthony Bedford Jnr, Jamahl Bedford, Kesha Bedford, Jessie Bradshaw, Lyndell Bradshaw, Jasirah Bin Hitam, Sumsuden Bin Rashid, Tatjana Bin Rashid, Terrick Bin Sali, Lehm Bradshaw, Dean Brown, Caen Chantanalgi, Jahli Currie, Trinity Currie, Stephen Dann Jnr, Aleiah Davey, Dennis Davey Jnr, Derek Davey Jnr, Ginju Davey Jnr, Hakeem Davey, Henry Davey Jnr, Jarron Davey, Johalia Davey, Keilan Davey, Margaret Davey, Maureen Davey, Sharnae Davey, Shikerha Davey, Vanden Davey, Cohen Dean, Rosanna Dean, Kivarne Dolby, Shania Dolby, Jeda Dudley, Sakara Edgar, Zarak Edgar, Junior Ejai, Kaleisha Ejai, Kamus Ejai, Sunjay Ejai, Isiah Goonack, Zacariah Green, Caleb Hankinson, Donald Hasslington, Jamahl Hasslington, Christopher Hubert Jnr, Marietta Hubert, Anfernee Hunter, Dereace Hunter, Giovanni Hunter, Memphis Hunter, Rodney Hunter, Salwyn Hunter, Taeisha Hunter, Wesley Hunter Jnr, Brehanna Isaac, Shailyn Isaac, Enid Ketchell, Darren Kirkman Jnr, Chenoa Maher, Jake Maher, Djuan Maher, Joeisha Maher, Jye Maher, Khe'Sanh Maher, Rodney Maher Jnr, Sharnee Maher, Sidonie Maher, William Maher Jnr, Yasmine Maher, Frederick Maru Jnr, Elijah Matthews, Nicole Mills, Ruby Marchioni, Miranda Maru, Amelia Matthews, Quanysha McCarthy, Tamara McCarthy, Kiaysha McHugh, Zena McHugh, Charlotte Mitchell, Christine Mitchell, Liam Mitchell, Nathaniel Mogridge, Karen Morgan, Manton Morgan, Dan Morris, Jeffrey Newry Jnr, Nikita O'Meara, Tyreece Parriman, Liam Powdrill, Rosharri Powdrill, Capel Price, Charli Price, Reid Price, Rosharn Puruntatameri, Tiahara Puruntatameri, Kieren Ryder, Waylon Sampi, Keith Sebastian, Matthew Sebastian Jnr, Asher Stone, Jayden Stone, Kirra-Lee Stone, Shoshana Stone, Jezeril Uhl, Tamika Ware, Taylani Xavier.

ILLUSTRATION CREDITS

(*Listed by page number*)

Front cover: Joshua Angus Jnr, married turtle; Brehanna Isaac, striped fish; Yasmine Maher, shells; Karen Morgan, boat fishing; Rosharri Powdrill, hermit crabs; **Spine**: Jasirah Bin Hitam, willy wagtail; **Back cover**: Shania Dolby, boy holding blue-tongue lizard; Sidonie Maher, blue-ringed octopus; Zena McHugh, seagull tracks; **Imprint page**: Anfernee Hunter, sooty oystercatcher; Enid Ketchel, pied oystercatcher; **Imprint page and opposite**: Hakeem Davey, white-breasted sea eagle; **Opposite Imprint page**: Khe'sahn Maher, starfish; **Opposite Contents**: Anthony Bedford Jnr, middle hammerheads; Frederick Maru Jnr, golden-lined spinefoot; Liam Powdrill, bottom left hammerhead; Rosharri Powdrill, coral trout; **Opposite Contents and Contents**: Sumsuden Bin Rashid, puffer fish; Anfernee Hunter, dugong; **Contents**: Henry Davey Jnr, shell; **Opposite Introduction**: Maureen Davey, crab; Rosharri Powdrill, turtle; Capel Price, girl; **Introduction**: Khe'sahn Maher, gecko; **12–13**: Kaleisha Ejai, person hunting; **13**: Margaret Davey, orange crab; Karen Morgan, bluebone; **14**: Donald Heslington, puffer fish; Shania Dolby, golden-lined spinefoot (left); Darren Kirkman Jnr, golden-lined spinefoot (right); **16**: Shania Dolby, baler shell; **16–17**: Khe'Sanh Maher, red crab; **18**: Trinity Currie, crabs; **18–19**: Khe'Sanh Maher, snake; **20**: Joshua Angus Jnr, hunting turtle in a boat; Kivarne Dolby, little turtle; Quanysha McCarthy, blue turtles; **22–23**: Frederick Maru Jnr, golden-lined spinefoot; **23**: Bonnita Angus, brahminy kite and golden trevally; Joshua Angus Jnr, turtle; Jasirah Bin Hitam, white-breasted sea eagle; Terrick Bin Sali, green mud crab; Lyndall Bradshaw, pelican; Aleiah Davey, manta ray and jellyfish; Maureen Davey, estuary cod; Zarak Edgar, tiger shark; Sidonie Maher, blue-ringed octopus; Daniel Morris, blue-spotted stingray; Capel Price, porcupine fish; Reid Price, bluebone; **25**: Aleiah Davey, clown fish; Maureen Davey, estuary cod; Brehanna Isaac, striped fish; Shailyn Isaac, wedge-tailed eagle; Joeisha Maher, giant clam; Khe'Sanh Maher, multi-coloured fish; **27**: Kamus Ejai, monkey fish; **28**: Jye Maher, sooty oystercatcher; Reid Price, pied oystercatcher; Keiren Ryder, grey goshawk; **30**: Jasirah Bin Hitam, willy wagtail; **31**: Jessie Bradshaw, pandanus; **32**: Capel Price, pandanus; **34–35**: Sharnee Maher, golden-lined spinefoot; Reid Price, bluebone; **36**: Zarak Edgar, sharks; Shailyn Isaac, people fishing; Frederick Maru Jnr, golden-lined spinefoot; **39**: Aleiah Davey, hermit crab; Rosharn Puruntatameri, goanna; Teromah Stumpagee, snake; **40**: Maureen Davey, turtle; Kaleisha Ejai, seagull; Kamus Ejai, dingo, turtle tracks, kangaroo and snake tracks; Shailyn Isaac, dingo tracks; Sharnee Maher, human tracks; Frederick Maru Jnr, snake; Zena McHugh, kangaroo tracks and seagull tracks; **41**: Anthony Bedford Jnr, blue-tongue lizard tracks; Lyndell Bradshaw, sooty oystercatcher and sooty oystercatcher tracks; Shania Dolby, boy holding blue-tongue lizard; Rodney Hunter, emu; Keiren Ryder, bull; Jayden Stone, bull tracks and emu tracks; **42**: Kaleisha Ejai, wedge-tailed eagle; **43**: Maureen Davey, snake; **44**: Rosharri Powdrill, family; Jezeril Uhl, orange person; **47**: Caen Chantanalgi, red crab; Stephen Dann Jnr, trevally; Djuan Maher, blue sword fish; **48**: Caen Chantanalgi, red hammerhead; Kaleisha Ejai, blue-and-white shark; Zacariah Green, middle hammerhead; Zena McHugh, blue shark (bottom and top right); Waylon Sampi, hammerhead (top right); **49**: Joshua Angus Jnr, married turtle; **56**: Tiahara Puruntatameri, person fishing; **57**: Joshua Angus Jnr, hermit crabs; Aleiah Davey, hermit crabs; Quanysha McCarthy, hermit crabs; **58**: Jezeril Uhl, person with fish; **59**: Zena McHugh, bough shelter; **60**: Chenoa Maher, background fish; Karen Morgan, boat fishing; **61**: Manton Morgan, Spanish flag; Capel Price, girl (top).